the ne minute mother

Other titles in this series:

the One minute mother

how to help your children learn to like themselves

SPENCER JOHNSON

HarperCollins*Publishers*

HarperCollins*Publishers*
77–85 Fulham Palace Road,
Hammersmith, London W6 8JB

www.harpercollins.co.uk

Published in the UK by HarperCollins*Publishers* 2004

Spencer Johnson asserts the moral right to
be identified as the author of this work

ISBN 13: 978-0-007-19142-0

The Symbol

The One Minute Mother's symbol—a one-minute readout from the face of a modern digital watch—is intended to remind each of us to take a minute out of our day, every now and then, and look into the faces of our children.

Dedicated to
my mother

and my sons

Emerson and Cameron

 *Contents*

A Letter to Mothers:

You certainly know from your own experience that being a good mother takes more than a minute.

However, there are ways you can communicate with your children—in only a minute—that will help them quickly learn how to like themselves and want to behave themselves.

The techniques are so simple, it may be difficult for you to believe that they will work.

Nonetheless, you may want to do as other parents have successfully done—suspend passing judgment on the three communications methods you're going to read about until you have actually used them in your own home for one month.

Then judge for yourself. See how your children's behavior improves. And ask your children how good they feel about themselves.

I'm sure you will find what I and other practical parents have found with our children: From both the children's and the parent's point of view, it works!

SPENCER JOHNSON, M.D.

The One Minute Mother

ONCE there was a bright young woman who was looking for an effective mother.

She wanted to learn the practical secrets of good parenting. And she knew she would find them only from someone who actually lived them.

The pregnant young woman had talked it over with her husband. They agreed that neither of them had ever really been taught how to raise children. Yet they would soon have a child of their own.

And so they decided to educate themselves, each in his or her own way.

The young woman took a leave of absence from her job. While she waited for her baby to arrive, she asked other mothers how they raised their children.

Over the next several months, she spoke with many women: young and old; traditional housewives and women who worked outside their homes; some with many children, others with only one child; married and single parents; mothers of toddlers and teenagers; those who took their parenting too seriously and those who had kept their sense of humor.

The young woman was beginning to see the many ways that women raise their children.

She noticed how much the mothers she spoke with cared about their children. She saw how hard they tried to be good mothers.

She often saw, however, what so many others did not want to see—the results of poor parenting: the common defiance or indifference in the children's eyes; the sorrow and frustration in the parents'. She didn't like a good deal of what she saw.

But she knew there was a better way.

She knew the results of good parenting were love and peace and joy in the home—for parents and children alike.

And she was determined to find it.

She had seen many women who had appeared to be "tough" parents—those who strictly disciplined their children.

Because they were such firm and consistent disciplinarians, some of these women's friends thought they were very good mothers.

Many of their children thought otherwise.

As the young woman sat in the homes of these "tough" parents, she asked, "What kind of a parent would you say you are?"

Their answers varied only slightly.

"I'm a conservative parent," the visitor was told. "I'm old-fashioned." "Traditional."

She heard the pride in their voices and their interest in their children's good behavior.

The young woman also met many apparently "nice" mothers who seemed to consider their children's feelings above everything else.

Because they appeared to be so understanding and sympathetic, some people thought they were very good mothers.

Their children, however, felt very differently about them.

As the young woman sat and listened to these "nice" mothers answer the same question, "What kind of a parent are you?" she heard, "I'm a modern parent." "Understanding." "Supportive."

She heard the pride in their voices and their interest in their children's self-esteem.

But she was disturbed.

It was as though most mothers in the world were primarily interested either in their children's behavior *or* in their children's self-esteem—one or the other.

The mothers who were interested in getting good behavior from their children were often referred to as "authoritarian" parents, while those who wanted self-esteem for their children were often referred to as "permissive" parents.

The young woman thought each of these mothers—the authoritarian and the permissive— was only partially effective. She knew each of these women was trying her best, based on what she knew how to do. "But," she thought, "it seems like being *half* a mother."

She continued to speak with other mothers— some in neighboring towns—but to no avail. She returned home from her search, tired and discouraged.

The young woman might have given up her search for an effective mother long ago, but she still had one great advantage. She knew exactly what she was looking for.

She told her husband later, "A truly effective mother somehow knows how to have the best of all worlds. She knows how to teach her children to like themselves *and* to behave themselves.

"And perhaps most important, she knows how to enjoy *herself* in the process."

Finally, as the young woman continued to talk to others, she began hearing marvelous stories about an active and interesting woman. In her older age, this woman was enjoying her life. She always seemed to find time for everything.

What caught the young woman's ear as she listened was the fact that the older woman was also a Special Mother—a woman who had an incredibly simple and effective method of child-rearing.

The Special Mother she heard about had raised three marvelous children with seemingly little effort. Each child had apparently been a well-behaved youngster and had since grown into a well-adjusted, prosperous, and happy adult.

Each of the older woman's three grown daughters had children of her own. And they were using the same parenting system with the same success.

The young woman wondered if these stories could really be true. And if so, she wondered if this mother would be willing to share her secrets with her.

She found the number in the telephone book and called her.

"I've heard that you have a very effective parenting system," the young woman said. "I wonder if I might come over and speak with you?"

"Of course," replied The Mother. "I'm flattered. I'd be happy to see you anytime."

WHEN the young woman arrived at The Mother's home, she expected to meet a "grandmother." Instead, she was welcomed by a vibrant, attractive woman who looked much younger than her years. The expectant mother wondered, "Could her parenting method have something to do with it?"

After they were comfortable over a cup of tea, The Mother asked, "Now, how can I help you?"

The young woman hesitated and then said, "I understand that you did a wonderful job of raising your children—and that you did this through a very special parenting approach."

The Mother responded with a smile. "I am very proud of my children. Each has grown up to become a happy, capable adult."

As the young woman began to relax, she opened her notebook and asked, "Do you mind if I take some notes?"

The Mother laughed and said, "Not at all—that is, as long as you realize that I do not have all the answers and that I was never a perfect mother.

"I just learned a few small secrets," The Mother suggested, "but they really made a very big improvement in our lives."

The visitor was anxious to know what they were. "Maybe we could start with discipline," she said. "A lot of parents tell me this is difficult. How did you discipline your children?"

"I didn't," The Mother replied.

The startled visitor asked, "What?"

The Mother smiled and said, "I didn't really discipline my children. I simply helped them to discipline themselves.

"That way," The Mother added with a nod, "it's a lot less tiring."

"Oh, then you're a permissive mother," the young woman suggested.

"No, not really," The Mother said. "I just believe that good parenting should not be exhausting. I'm afraid permissive parenting can make for unruly children. And such children will exhaust any parent."

The young visitor said, trying to sound as knowledgeable as possible, "So you are aware of the need for good behavior. Then you are more behavior-oriented than you are self-esteem–oriented."

The Mother sat forward and said quietly, "I hear that sort of talk all too often. It's like which came first—the chicken or the egg?—a child's good behavior or a child's good self-image?

"As complicated as parenting may seem to many of us at times," The Mother said, "the basic answer really can be quite simple."

The Mother rose and went to her desk. She picked up something and returned. "Here, look at this," she said, as she handed her visitor a plaque.

"When my children were young, I always kept this nearby to remind me of a very basic truth about parenting."

*

*Children Who
Like Themselves*

*Like To
Behave Themselves*

*

"Once you know this simple truth," The Mother said, "it becomes easier to deal with your children."

The visitor asked, "Is this really that important?"

The woman smiled and said, "It is the most basic idea behind the way I parent. In fact, it can make the difference between whether a family feels blessed or stressed."

Then The Mother let the young woman discover the answer for herself. "The best way to find the truth is to ask yourself, 'Is this compatible with my *own* life's experiences?'

"Think about your own childhood," The Mother gently encouraged her. "Then ask yourself, 'When did I behave best? When I felt good about myself? Or when I didn't?'"

The young woman nodded, as she began to see. "I guess," she said, "now that I think of it, I acted best when I felt good about myself."

"Of course!" exclaimed The Mother delightedly. "We all do."

The young woman got up from her chair and carried the plaque back to the desk. She stood there for a moment thinking deeply.

"So," she said, "helping children feel good about themselves is a key to getting good behavior from them. Is that what you are saying?"

"Yes," replied The Mother. "And the good news is that when you help your children like themselves, they help you by doing better."

The young woman's interest increased. "You have already said that you are not a permissive mother. How then," she asked The Mother, "would you describe yourself?"

"That's easy," she responded with a smile. "I'm a 'One Minute Mother.'"

The young woman's face showed surprise. She'd obviously never heard of a One Minute Mother. She asked incredulously, "You're a what?"

The woman laughed. "My children call me that. I know, of course, that it takes a lot more than just one minute to be a good mother.

"But more important, it reminds me of three ways of communicating with my children—each of which takes only a minute or so. These three simple communication techniques certainly helped my children learn how to like themselves—and want to behave themselves."

"It sounds too good to be true!" the expectant mother said.

"I know," The Mother smiled. "I felt that way when I first met a parent in our neighborhood many years ago. They called him 'The One Minute Father.' He was the one who first told me about the three one-minute communication secrets.

"But I tried them for myself and they worked. I found with experience, however, that a mother's approach was somewhat different from a father's," the woman said. "So I simply adapted them a little to work better for me as a mother."

"But you're saying that the same three secrets will work just as well for fathers," the visitor suggested, "although in a little different way."

"Absolutely," The Mother assured her visitor.

The young woman said, "My husband will be very glad to hear that. He's also talking with people and reading books to try to find out how to be a good father."

The young woman smiled and added, "I guess you can tell it's our first."

"I hope you don't have to learn by trial and error," The Mother suggested, "the way I did.

"I've finally discovered that good parenting doesn't have to be complicated. In fact, I've learned from my own experiences that really good parenting is simple, fun, and enjoyable—both for the parents *and* for the children."

The young woman felt an exhilaration. This was what she was looking for! The anxious young woman asked, "What are these three secrets?"

"Rather than ask me," The Mother responded, "perhaps you could learn more by talking with my grown children. They know better than anyone whether or not it is good for the children themselves to have a One Minute Mother."

The Mother asked for a piece of paper from the young woman's notebook and wrote on it. "Here are their names and telephone numbers."

"Thank you," the young woman said. "I would like very much to talk with your daughters.

"May I ask one thing, however, before I go?

"When you said that these were three 'secrets,' did you mean that these were three parenting techniques you were using on your children without their knowledge?"

"No, quite the opposite. Calling them secrets is just my dry sense of humor. Each of these secrets of communication is something most of us already somehow sense. But since so few of us use what we know, you'd think they were secrets.

"The real benefits, of course, come to us when, as parents, we take our common sense and use it in our homes as common practice.

"No," The Mother said. "I did not hide anything from my children. As most of us know from personal experience, things work better when you are up-front with people. It avoids a *lot* of problems.

"I told my children that I did not want to manipulate them. And I did not want them to manipulate me. I think what I said was 'I don't want to be a dictator or a doormat.'

"I told my children about the three methods before I began to use them. I described them simply as common sense.

"And then I encouraged my children to use the same three methods of communication with me.

"I finally learned the hard way," she added, "that communicating with children is like driving a car on a two-way street: It works best when things flow freely in both directions.

"So please remember when you are learning the three secrets," The Mother cautioned, "that they work best when you also encourage the children to exercise their rights as people—to communicate with you what *they* think and feel as well."

"Thank you," the visitor said. "I will." She stood up, shook hands with her hostess, and left.

As the young woman sat alone in her car, she looked through her notebook and saw the names of the three daughters. She looked forward to talking with each one of them: Patricia Gavin, Susan Saunders, and Elizabeth Franklin.

THAT evening the young woman was welcomed into the home of William and Patricia Gavin and their three children—two sons, sixteen and twelve, and a nine-year-old daughter.

When their guest arrived, the children were busily playing a noisy video game with their equally noisy father as referee.

Introductions were made all around. Then Will and the children excused themselves and left the two women alone to talk quietly.

Pat Gavin was cheerful and relaxed. Like her mother, she seemed happy with herself. And she too looked younger than her years.

"I understand you've spent some time with my mother," the daughter said. "She's quite a woman, isn't she?"

"To tell you the truth, Mrs. Gavin," the visitor responded, "I really wasn't with her very long."

"Please call me Pat," the daughter said. "And take it from someone who knows. She really is a marvelous woman! Did she tell you about being a One Minute Mother?"

"She sure did. It's not true, is it? I mean, she reminded me that it takes more than a minute to be a good mother. But did she *really* spend so little time parenting and still get such great results?"

"Well, it certainly took her very little time," the daughter confirmed. "I understand that you are meeting with both of my sisters as well as with me." She smiled and said, "So, I'll let you judge the results for yourself."

The young woman appreciated the daughter's not trying to "sell" her. She asked, "Did you feel that you got *enough* of your mother's time?"

The daughter thought for a moment and then said, "I remember when my father died. We were all young but my mother still had to go to work to support the family. None of us had as much time with her as we would have enjoyed."

Then she added, "Nonetheless, I *did* feel I got enough time. What I remember most clearly is that the time she spent with me made me feel special."

"Can you give me an example of how she made you feel special?" the young woman asked.

"Yes. When I was learning something new, for instance, she always made me feel capable."

"How did she do that?" the young woman inquired.

"To begin with," the daughter said, "she would sit down at our dining-room table and do One Minute Goal Setting with me."

"One Minute Goal Setting?" the young woman inquired. "Your mother told me she was a One Minute Mother, but she never said anything about One Minute Goal Setting. What is that?"

"That's the first of the three secrets to One Minute Parenting," the daughter announced.

"Three secrets?"

"Yes," said the daughter. "One Minute Goal Setting is the first one and the foundation of One Minute Parenting.

"Unfortunately, many parents know too little about it. For instance, when you ask most parents and children what they each think their goals are and then compare their answers, what do you think you find?"

The visitor laughed and said, "Pat, in some of the families I've visited, any relationship between what the children thought their goals were and what the parents thought was purely coincidental."

"Of course," the daughter said. "Problems constantly arise because people are not clear about what the other family members want."

The young woman nodded. She remembered her own childhood. She remembered how often that had happened to her and how painful it had been. Then she asked, "Does that ever happen with your family?"

"Practically never. The One Minute Mother helps her children understand what their goals are."

Then she added, "One of the greatest things about my mother is that she also taught me *how* to become a One Minute Mother."

It was just what the young woman wanted to know. "Just how does a woman do that?" she asked.

"Efficiently," the daughter said with a smile.

She went on to explain.

"To begin with, we use One Minute Goals. They are simply the things we would like to see happening in our family, written down in fewer than two hundred and fifty words, on a single sheet of paper."

"You write down your goals?"

"Yes," the woman responded. "It's very important. People who have written goals realize them far more often than those who don't."

"I see," said the young woman, as she wrote down her own notes. "But why are your goals written in fewer than two hundred and fifty words on a single sheet of paper?"

"So that we can each read and review our goals in only a minute."

"Why is that important?" the visitor asked.

"Because the more quickly we can review our goals, the more frequently we do it," the daughter explained. "The more *often* we review our goals, the sooner they become a routine way of thinking—a regular part of our family life."

The visitor took note: *Because they take only a minute to review, they are called "One Minute Goals."* As she wrote in her notebook, she asked, "Can you give me some specific examples?"

"Well, there are two kinds of goals—'We' goals and 'I' goals. 'We' goals are shared by two or more members of the family; 'I' goals are those of a single family member.

"For example, several years ago, we were having a tough time getting our son to go to bed on time. It was often a hassle, with tears and yelling."

"So what did you do?"

"My husband and my son Billy and I took about an hour one evening to work it out. We all agreed that we wanted two things: first, for Billy and for us to enjoy ourselves at night and second, to feel good—that is, rested—in the morning. That became our goal.

"He was so young," the woman noted, "that in order to have it written down, we helped Billy draw a happy face at night, then a sleeping face, then a happy face in the morning. We encouraged him to look at it each night after dinner.

"Then we agreed to a plan and I wrote it down. We later read this to Billy for the first few nights. It took only a minute: Billy would go to bed at seven-thirty on weeknights. He could leave his light on and look at a book or do whatever he wanted to do in bed until we told him that it was eight o'clock. We would get him an alarm clock and he would be responsible for getting up on time without complaining. On weekends, he could stay up two hours later, unless he had to get up early the next morning, in which case he would have to go to bed as though it were a weekday."

"And did it work?" the visitor asked.

"Usually," the woman answered. "He felt that he had a voice in what happened and that it was fair."

"What did you do, Pat, when it didn't work?"

"That's the third secret," she said with a smile. "We'll get to that later."

"Fine," the young woman responded, trying her best to be patient. "If that was a 'We' goal, can you give me an example of an 'I' goal?"

"Let's ask Billy," replied his mother. "He's grown up a lot since we drew pictures for him." She excused herself and returned with her son.

The twelve-year-old boy said hello and handed the visitor his list of goals. There were two. *1) I am going to be able to afford to go on a school ski trip February 2nd by working hard to make $150. 2) I am making a B on my math test May 5th by studying math every day for at least 30 minutes.*

The visitor asked the boy, "How do you like the idea of writing down your goals?"

"At first," the boy said, "I didn't like it. It seemed like kind of a waste of time to me. But now I like doing it whenever I really want something."

"Why do you like doing it now?"

He laughed and said, "Because it helps me get what I want!" The boy and the visitor talked for a while. They liked one another. Later he asked to be excused and left.

The visitor turned to the boy's mother and said, "I don't understand. Why do you all write your goals as though you had already achieved them?"

"Remember, I said that 'goals are what we want to see happen,'" she answered. "Well, in our family we mentally 'see' them *before* they happen.

"By writing out our goals as though we were already realizing them, we use a secret that many other successful people have used in their lives. And we are discovering the same thing: it works!

"Most of the time we achieve most of our goals."

"Let me just see if I understand it," the young woman said. "You write down what you would like to see happen, what you are specifically doing about it, and the date by which you would like to have realized your goal. And then you review this often."

"Yes. We have seen that the more often we write out what we want and regularly review it, the more often we get what we want.

"In fact," the woman added, "in order to support one another we each keep a copy of the other person's goals."

"Isn't this a lot of paperwork?"

"No, it really isn't," the woman insisted. "As The One Minute Mother pointed out to me so often when I was growing up, only about twenty percent of what any of us does gives us practically eighty percent of our results. So in our family we do One Minute Goal Setting only on our important twenty percent. Of course, in the event something special comes up, we may set a special One Minute Goal for ourselves. But it is always on a single piece of paper."

"It seems a very efficient way to do it," the visitor said. "I think I understand the importance of One Minute Goal Setting. It sounds like a system of 'no surprises'—everyone knows what is important to the other members of the family."

"Exactly," the woman agreed.

"Do you assume," the young woman asked, "that your children will know how to do what they have agreed to do?"

"No," the woman said. "Once the children know what their responsibilities for good behavior are, we show them what good behavior looks like."

"For example?"

"If their responsibility, let's say, is to clean their rooms, and part of that is to make their beds, then I first show them how to make the bed—slowly and carefully."

"Doesn't that take a lot of time?" the visitor wanted to know.

"Only at first," the daughter insisted. "But the time I invest in the beginning pays off handsomely. When children, or anyone else for that matter, first get to see how something is done properly and to know what standard is expected of them, you are helping them avoid failure."

"You mean it keeps you out of constant 'Rescue and Salvage' operations the rest of the time?"

"It really does," the woman said. "But not completely. Sometimes my younger children need to be reminded of their agreements."

The visitor thought for a moment and then said, "You mentioned earlier than only twenty percent of the activities brought eighty percent of the results you were looking for. How do you know what the important twenty percent is?"

The woman rose to her feet and began to walk about her living room. She asked her visitor, "Would you care for anything else to eat or drink?" When she received a polite, "No thank you," she continued to walk about slowly. Pat Gavin was obviously a woman deep in thought. It was as though she had been thinking about the very same point herself recently.

"You ask good questions. You can figure out for yourself what your twenty percent is when you learn how to W.I.N.—that is, to ask yourself, 'What's Important Now?'"

"I used to have 'To Do' lists," the woman said. "They would depress me because I never seemed to get everything done.

"Now I've discovered an easy way to know what I ought to be doing. I *preview* the day—or the week, month, year, whatever—by asking myself, 'What is most important?' And then I *review* by asking myself, 'Did I do the most important?'"

The visitor looked excited and said, "If you didn't get the important things done that day, it's easy to see what you need to do the next day. And if you got the important things done, it doesn't matter that you didn't do all the other things."

"Precisely," the woman said.

"It all comes back to having One Minute Goals. In fact," she added, "let me show you a plaque that I keep on my desk so that I can read it each morning before my day begins."

*

I Take A Minute
I Look At My Goals
I Look At My Behavior

I See If My Behavior
Matches My Goals

*

The young woman handed the plaque back and asked, "When you say that you actually look at your behavior, do you actually look at something—like your appointment calendar?"

"That's exactly what I mean."

"That's marvelous," the visitor said. "May I make a copy of this idea?" she asked.

"Of course," the daughter responded. "I hope you *use* it.

"I learned most of what I know about One Minute Parenting from someone else, namely, my mother, and I am happy to share it with you."

The woman added, "I look at my goals at least once a day and I encourage my children to do the same. Then on Saturday mornings, we briefly review our goals and our progress as a family. It makes quite a difference."

The young woman began writing in her notebook as quickly as she could. Then she paused and said, "If I may, I'd like to take just a few minutes to write a summary of what I have learned about One Minute Goal Setting."

"Of course," the daughter said. "I'll be in the kitchen. Just call when you're done."

Being a quick learner, the young woman wrote her notes as though she were already using the method herself.

One Minute Goals work well for our family when:

1. We have clear goals as a family ("We" goals), and as individuals ("I" goals).

2. We strive for mutual agreement so we all feel we are getting what we want from the family.

3. We each write out our goals in 250 words or fewer, on a single piece of paper—so it takes us only a minute or so to reread them.

4. Our goals are *specific*, showing exactly what we would each like to see happen and when. *I have . . . I am doing . . . It has happened by . . .*

5. We each *reread* our goals often in order to make them mental habits—a way of thinking.

6. I take a minute out every now and then. I look at my own goals. I look at my behavior. I see if my behavior matches my goals.

7. I encourage my children to do the same.

8. Once a week, we enjoy reviewing our goals and progress together as a family.

Shortly after the visitor had written her summary, The One Minute Mother's daughter returned. "Do you have any other questions?"

"Just one more, Pat. How," she asked, "do you get your children to *want* to have goals?"

Before she could answer, the woman's nine-year-old daughter, Amy, entered the room and said, "Excuse me, Mom, but I've finished my homework. Can Jeanne come over now and play for a while?"

As she was leaving with permission, the visitor asked, "Amy, what does a goal mean to you?"

"Oh, that's easy," the youngster responded. She had been studying and had found the answers to much harder questions.

"A goal is a dream with a deadline."

As the woman watched her child go off to play, she said fondly, "That is a good part of the answer. My sons and daughter *enjoy* having dreams. And if you're wondering how that happens, you will want to know about the second secret of One Minute Parenting."

"And what is that?" the young woman asked. She looked at her watch.

The woman smiled. "I understand that you are having lunch tomorrow with my sister Susan. I'll let her tell you." The woman walked her visitor to the door.

"Thank you for your time," the young woman said.

"You're welcome. I have time now. As you can probably tell, I've become a One Minute Mother."

The visitor left, looking forward to tomorrow.

AS the young woman drove to the home of The One Minute Mother's second daughter, she thought about the simplicity of what she had learned the previous night. She thought, "It certainly makes sense. And what a clear and easy way to help children clarify things for themselves.

"I would think it would help children learn about both commitment and responsibility."

The young woman wondered, as she walked up to the apartment building, why Susan Saunders had suggested such a late lunch. She soon found out. The second daughter told her that she was in a work/study program every morning and was raising two children—a boy, eleven, and a girl, four. She liked to be home when the children were.

"It's nice of you to have me for lunch and to explain One Minute Parenting," the visitor said.

"I'm happy to," the second daughter responded. "If more mothers used the three simple secrets of One Minute Parenting, there would be more happy families, enjoyable neighborhoods, and better communities. I really mean that! I do!"

Then the daughter laughed and said, "I get carried away." The gleam in her eye reflected her personal happiness. The visitor felt good in this mother's presence. They enjoyed a leisurely lunch.

The daughter said later, "I understand you've been to see Mom. She's quite a woman, isn't she?"

The young woman was already getting used to The One Minute Mother's being called "quite a woman."

"I guess she is," responded the cautious young woman. "What is it that you especially liked so much about your mother and the way she raised you?"

"I liked a lot of things. But one of the best is that my sisters and I always knew where we stood with Mom. We knew specifically what was expected of us and we knew we were loved. For a kid, that's a pretty secure feeling."

"Yes, your sister Pat told me all about One Minute Goals."

"Well, actually I was thinking about One Minute *Praisings*," the woman said.

"One Minute Praisings?" the visitor asked. "Are they the second secret to becoming a One Minute Mother?"

"Yes, they are. In fact, I believe that The One Minute Mother's second secret is the *most* powerful technique of all."

The visitor sat forward and pulled out her notebook.

"It's very simple," the woman began. "Mother told me early that it would be a lot easier for me to do well in life if I knew how I was doing. And so she said that she was going to let me know *in no uncertain terms* when she did not like what I was doing and when she did.

"And she said she wanted us to do the same with her.

"And then she cautioned me that it might not be comfortable for either of us."

"Why?" the visitor wanted to know.

"The One Minute Mother knows that it is not comfortable at first for either children or parents."

"Why is that?"

"Because, as she pointed out, most parents don't treat their children that way and most children aren't used to it. But I remember her assuring me that such feedback would be a big help to me. And she said that my doing it to her would also help her."

"There is another thing you should know. Mom cautioned me not to expect her always to do things well. Sometimes she was tired or had something else important on her mind. And she would forget to do the second secret."

"In other words," the visitor said, "The One Minute Mother was like all the rest of us. We all let down and we all make mistakes."

"Of course," the daughter answered. "But the point is, when she did remember to do the second secret, it worked wonders with us."

"Can you please tell me exactly how it works?"

"Yes, of course. Shortly after my mother did One Minute Goal Setting with me, she would sometimes watch me more closely than usual."

"What was she watching for?" the young woman wanted to know.

"She was trying to catch me doing something right."

"Catch you doing something *right*?" echoed the visitor.

"Yes. In fact, we have a motto in each of our families that says:

*

*I Help My Children
Reach Their
Full Potential*

*I Catch Them
Doing Something
Right*

*

Susan Saunders continued, "In most families, the parents spend too much of their time catching children doing what?"

The young woman smiled and said knowingly, "Doing something wrong."

The woman said, "Here we catch each other doing something right."

The young woman made several notes and then asked, "What do you *do,* Susan, when you catch your children doing something right?"

"That's when I give them a One Minute Praising," the woman said with some delight.

"What does that mean?" the young woman wanted to know.

"Well, when I see that one of the children has done something that makes me feel exceptionally good, I go over to him, and put my arm around him, look into his face and say two things: First, I tell him specifically what he has *done,* and second, I tell him exactly how I *feel* about it. I let a few seconds of silence pass between us to allow him to *feel* how good I am feeling."

Just then, the women heard a door slam. The One Minute Mother's daughter said, "Excuse me," as she turned and called to her child. "Jimmy, did you get it?"

"Yeah, Mom."

"Well, bring it here, honey. I'm anxious to see it." There was no answer. Susan Saunders called out again. "Jimmy, are you all right? Was everything OK at school?"

It seemed forever before her eleven-year-old son came slowly into the living room. He handed his mother the report card. She studied it carefully.

The boy began to fidget. He knew what was on it—two A's, three B's, and a D. He got the D in history.

"James Saunders," she began slowly. She paused. She looked again at the report. Then she exclaimed, "You're terrific!"

The boy grinned.

"Just look at this!" she said enthusiastically. "You got two A's and three B's on your report card!"

She put her arms around her boy and said, "I am very happy, Jimmy. I feel good about your success."

The boy gave her a quick hug and then he seemed embarrassed. "Can I go out and play?" he asked. "Just for a little while?"

The woman smiled and said to her child, "Anyone who gets practically all A's and B's on his report card can go out and play all afternoon."

The boy's grin widened. He disappeared behind "Thanks, Mom" and a slamming door. Then he came back in briefly and said, "I love you, Mom."

The amazed young woman looked at where the boy had been a moment ago and said, "I don't understand. Your child just brought home a D on his report card."

"Yes. I'm afraid he did."

"But," the visitor protested, "you didn't say anything about the D."

"You noticed."

The visitor couldn't help but smile. Then she laughed and said, "I noticed."

Soon the visitor became serious again. She was obviously concerned. "But isn't it irresponsible not even to mention the D he got in history?"

"Irresponsible on whose part?" the mother inquired.

"Well, on your part," the visitor suggested.

The woman said gently, "I am not taking history this year."

The visitor was startled. Then she said, "I know your child is taking the course, but isn't it your responsibility to help your child get good grades?"

"No," the woman answered, "that is my child's responsibility. If I assume his responsibility, my child never will."

She continued, "You might want to think about what the word *responsibility* means. It means just that: 'response ability'—the ability to respond.

"One of the greatest gifts I can give my children is to let them be *alive*—to let them respond to life. I help each of my children *enjoy* assuming his or her own responsibilities."

"How?" the young woman asked.

"The best way to have my children assume their own responsibilities is to let them discover how good it feels."

"And how do you do that?" the visitor asked.

"You just saw it," the daughter of The One Minute Mother pointed out. "Right now, my son is assuming responsibility for his A's and B's. He is experiencing the consequences of getting good grades. First, he feels good and I feel good. He will play and enjoy himself all afternoon. There will be no chores or homework today. It's a special day of celebration."

"So," the visitor said, reflecting on what she was hearing, "your children learn that assuming responsibility is something they *get* to do instead of something they *have* to do."

"Well said! You're catching on. And since I can anticipate your next question, I might as well answer it. What do I do about the D?" The visitor nodded her appreciation.

"I'll help my child learn by posing several simple questions to him the way Socrates used to teach Greek children. I'll ask Jimmy how good he felt about his A's and B's; what grade he would like to get in history; if he thinks he can do it; what his plan is to get it, et cetera."

The visitor asked, "Will you do that this Saturday morning—at the family goal-setting session?"

"Yes," the woman confirmed. "And what do you think Jimmy is likely to say? In fact," she added, "how do you think he went from getting mostly C's to mostly A's and B's?"

The visitor suggested, "I think he's discovering how good he feels when he gets good grades. So I suspect that he will want to do better in history—simply because he likes the feeling of success."

"Precisely!" the woman confirmed. "And that is the practical power of receiving a One Minute Praising. In fact, more often than not, the inner response is 'If you think that's good, folks, wait'll you see my next act.'"

The visitor smiled and the woman added, "When my children are caught doing something right, they want to do something right again. It makes *them* feel good about themselves. And children who like themselves like to behave themselves."

"So instead of behaving for *you*," the visitor observed, "they are doing it for themselves."

"Yes. And that is critical to good parenting. Of course, Jimmy's father and I will help him all we can when he sets his goals for a good grade in history. But our real secret is to help each of our children *want* to do well."

"And when they do well, you let them enjoy their success by praising them for it."

The visitor added, "Instead of ignoring good behavior, the way too many of us do with one another."

"Now you've got it," the woman said.

"Let me just make a summary of what I've learned," the young woman said. She wrote in her notebook. Again, she wrote her notes as though she were already using the One Minute Praising.

One Minute Praisings work well when:

1. I tell my children *beforehand* that I am going to praise them when they do well.

2. I catch my children doing something *right.*

3. I tell my children specifically what they *did.*

4. I tell them how good I *feel* about what they did.

5. I stop and let a few seconds of silence pass to let *them* feel how good I feel.

6. Then I do what genuinely matches my feelings right then. I tell them I *love* them or give them a *hug*, or both.

7. I later encourage my children to do the same for me—to catch me doing something right and to give me a praising.

8. I realize that while it takes me only a minute to praise my children, their feeling good about themselves may last them for a *lifetime.*

9. I know that what I am doing is good for my children and for me. I feel really good about *myself* as a parent.

The visitor looked up from her notebook and said, "Thank you. This is very valuable. I can see now why you say the second secret is so powerful."

Then the visitor asked anxiously, "What's the third secret?"

Susan smiled at her visitor's enthusiasm, rose from her chair, and said, "Why don't you ask my older sister, Liz? I understand that you are seeing her later."

"Yes, I am," the visitor admitted. "Well, thank you so much for your time."

"That's OK," insisted the daughter. "Since I have become a One Minute Mother, I have time."

The visitor smiled. She'd heard that someplace before.

As the young woman left the home of The One Minute Mother's second child, she realized how much she liked Susan Saunders. "What a marvelous way to live," she thought. "How much more enjoyable it is to catch people doing something *right*."

What she had learned from two of The One Minute Mother's daughters made a lot of sense to her. "But," she wondered, "do One Minute Goals and One Minute Praisings really work?"

As she drove away, her curiosity about results increased. She stopped at a telephone booth and changed her appointment with the third daughter.

There was something more important she wanted to do first. She wanted to find out for herself.

THE next day the young woman returned to The One Minute Mother's neighborhood. She walked along the tree-lined street enjoying a beautiful Saturday morning. The young woman was impressed by the area's cleanliness and the friendly greetings from those she passed. It gave her courage to do what she had come to do.

She stood in front of one house and hesitated. Then she went up and knocked on the door. A man answered. "What can I do for you?" he asked.

"You can talk with me, if you will," the young woman requested. She introduced herself and said, "I am expecting my first child and I am trying to learn more about being a good parent. I have been speaking with the lady who lives a few doors down, the lady they call 'The One Minute Mother'—and with her daughters Patricia and Susan. I was wondering if you might tell me what I want to know."

The man smiled and said, "I will if I can." He introduced himself as Steven Herrick and asked, "What would you like to know?"

"To come straight to the point," the young woman said, "I would like to know if her methods work. I mean, I wonder if you or any of the others in the neighborhood might know what her children were like growing up."

The man answered, "Well, I grew up with them. I know them very well. But I'm afraid I can't tell you much about their mother's method of raising them because I don't know much about it."

"What were the children like?"

"Well," he began, "they were very . . ." He hesitated and then said, ". . . alive. That's it." He spoke as though he were reliving a part of his childhood, talking almost to himself.

"They were active and interested in so many things. I remember little things now that I think about it. Like their looking on hot days through the blades of grass for a variety of little bugs they found there. They called them the signs of life. I remember their talking to old people for hours on end as though they were really listening and learning from them. I remember . . .

"You know, I didn't think much about it then, but I guess now that I look back on it, those kids were really something. They were really happy. Everybody in the neighborhood liked them."

"Tell me," the young woman said, "did they ever get into trouble?"

"Oh, sure!" the man told her.

"Aha," the young woman said, thinking she was on to something. "What happened then?"

"I don't know," the man said. "I wish I did. But I do remember one thing."

"What was that?"

"I remember that the girls seldom got into trouble for the same thing again." He added, "In fact I think some of the other mothers in the neighborhood were so impressed that they found out what The One Minute Mother did."

The man continued, "I wish I knew what The One Minute Mother's secrets were. I've been meaning to go over there, but I just haven't had the time.

"I must admit," he added, "I could use whatever help I could get with *my* kids. You know kids today." The woman said nothing.

Then the man added, "Perhaps I could even become a One Minute Father."

The young woman smiled and said, "I'm taking notes. So I'd be glad to give the three secrets as a gift when I find out the last one myself. Just as she is giving them to me."

The young woman thanked the man for speaking with her. She didn't understand *how* or *why* One Minute Parenting worked. But she was beginning to suspect that whatever it was, this apparently simple parenting system might just be very effective.

That night the young woman had a restless sleep. She found herself excited about the next day—about learning the third secret to becoming a One Minute Mother.

THE next morning the young woman was welcomed by The One Minute Mother's eldest daughter, Elizabeth Franklin, a single parent of a teenage son, and a woman who worked full time outside her home.

After she and her visitor had tasted their Sunday morning coffee, Elizabeth—who preferred to be called Liz—said, "I know you've been to see Mom. She's quite a woman, isn't she?"

The young woman was no longer surprised to hear this. She said, "Yes, she is!"

"I understand you want to know more about One Minute Parenting," the woman said. "What would you like to know?"

"Well," the young woman began, "yesterday I spoke with a man who lives in your old neighborhood. He told me that he knew you and Pat and Sue when you were growing up. He said that you and your sisters were like most children—you got into trouble occasionally—but that you were unlike most children because you seldom got into the same trouble again. I was wondering, Liz, if that was the result of something your mother did—something about the way she raised you and your sisters."

The woman laughed and said, "You'd better believe it!"

"Can you remember it well enough to tell me about it?" the young woman asked.

"Very easily," she said. "It's not the kind of thing one ever forgets!"

She went on to explain.

"Whenever I didn't keep a commitment to myself or my family, Mother would confirm the facts and review our goals with me—to be sure I clearly understood what I had agreed to.

"Then, when she knew I understood, she would give me a One Minute Reprimand."

"A what!" the startled young woman asked.

"A One Minute *Reprimand*," the young mother repeated.

"Is that the third secret to One Minute Parenting?"

"It is indeed! In fact, I think it's the third secret to better communication between *any* two people: parent and child, manager and employee, student and teacher—even husband and wife."

"Why is that?" the young woman asked.

"Because it's an effective way to deal with unpleasant situations between two people before things deteriorate into a bad relationship."

"How does it work?" wondered the visitor.

"It's simple," said the woman.

The young woman laughed and said, "I figured you'd say that."

Elizabeth Franklin smiled. She explained, "First, Mother had told me beforehand that she was going to let me know when I was doing something that was unacceptable to her. She assured me that the feedback she gave me would help me become a winner in my own right. In fact she used to say, *'Feedback Is the Breakfast of Champions.'* So whenever I did something that was unacceptable, Mother was quick to respond."

"What did she do?" the visitor asked.

"As soon as she learned about it, she made a point of coming to see me. She asked me to come to a private part of the house. Then she looked me straight in the eye, and told me precisely what I had *done*. Then she told me in no uncertain terms how she *felt* about it—angry, frustrated, annoyed, sad, disappointed, or whatever she was feeling.

"She would intensely say into my face, *'I am annoyed! Annoyed!'*

"After she told me rather emotionally just how she felt, she let what she said sink in with a few seconds of deadly silence. And, boy, did it sink in!"

"How long did that take?" asked the young woman.

"It lasted only about thirty seconds, but there were times when it seemed like forever. It was a very intense, emotional, upsetting, *unpleasant* experience!"

The young woman moved to the edge of her chair and asked, "And then what happened?"

"Then she would take a deep breath to relax herself. And then she put her hand on my shoulder to let me know she was on my side. When she spoke, it was in a softer tone of voice. She told me that my recent behavior was not acceptable, but that *I* was. She made sure that I knew the reason she was so upset with my behavior was that she knew I was *better* than that. She reminded me that I was very valuable and worthwhile.

"Then she gave me a big hug and said, 'I love you, honey!'"

The visitor noted, "That must have made you think twice—about your *behavior* and about *yourself.*"

"It certainly did!" confirmed the daughter.

The young woman was taking notes now as fast as she could. She sensed that it wasn't going to take this woman long to cover several important points.

"My mother's One Minute Reprimands made quite an impression on me because of the way she did them. First, she let me know as *soon* as I'd done something unacceptable. Second, since she told me *exactly* what I had done wrong, I knew that she was on top of things—I was not going to get away with much. Third, since she didn't attack *me* as a person, only my behavior, it was easier for me not to become defensive. I didn't try to justify my mistake by fixing blame on anyone else. I knew she was being fair. And fourth, I knew she cared about me and wanted me to feel really good about myself."

The daughter laughed and said, "Of course, that's what I think now. But I remember when I was a youngster and Mother first started to use the One Minute Reprimand. I really fought it.

"In fact, I did just about everything I could to get her to stop using it as a discipline with me. I put my hands over my ears, or I walked away, or I laughed and pretended I didn't care.

"But Mother just uncovered my ears, or followed me down the hall, or did whatever else was necessary. She always completed her Reprimand.

"Of course, I tried to interrupt her in the middle of the Reprimand—to tell her all the great reasons why I had done whatever I had done."

"In other words," the visitor suggested, "you got defensive. So what did your mother do?"

"First, while Mother made it clear that I wasn't going to get to talk to her during a Reprimand, she also let me know that I could come back several hours later and discuss anything I liked with her. She wanted me to listen to her.

"And she always said *the best way to get someone to listen to you is to listen to them.*

"However, when I had time to think it over, I usually realized that she had been fair and so I didn't go back to discuss it. It just helped to know that I could talk to her later if I wanted to.

"And perhaps most important, I stopped being defensive when I discovered that she attacked only my behavior and not my worth. I found that I didn't need to defend my behavior—because I never had to defend my personal worth.

"That's why, whenever I reprimand my own child," the daughter said, "I make sure that I do not destroy his belief in *himself*."

The visitor looked at the woman and said, "I think I'm beginning to understand. The result of the One Minute Reprimand is that you feel bad about your behavior but good about yourself. And the better you feel about yourself, the better your behavior becomes."

"Yes. That's a good summary," the woman said.

"Can you give me a specific example of a One Minute Reprimand?" the young woman asked.

"Certainly," agreed the woman. "I was having a very difficult time with my seventeen-year-old son, David, who was very resentful about my divorce from his father. I wasn't exactly in the best of shape then myself. And I wasn't using the three secrets of One Minute Parenting. Things got out of hand. He would take the car and stay out until all hours, and talk back to me when I tried to deal with him."

The visitor frowned and asked, "What did you do?"

"I began to use the One Minute Reprimand every time he came home late with the car."

"What did you say to him?"

"I went up to my son and told him something like this: 'David, you disobey me. You take the car without asking. It's now one-thirty in the morning! You come home whenever you want. You talk back to me when I speak to you about it. Your behavior is unacceptable! Absolutely unacceptable!'

"I then expressed what I had felt for so long— with full emotions and *in no uncertain terms.* I said: 'I am losing sleep. I worry about the car. I worry about you. I *resent* your behavior! I am *upset*! I am *angry*! I am *very angry*!'

"I put my angry face up next to his and let a few seconds of silence pass so that he could *feel* what I was feeling.

"Then I took a deep breath to compose myself, and lowered my voice. I touched my son to let him know I cared and said, 'You're better than this kind of behavior, David. I know you're resentful about the divorce. That's only human. And I know that you are a really good kid. I admire you, David, in so many ways. I love you, son.'

"Then I hugged him to let him know that the reprimand was over."

"And what happened?" the young woman asked.

"At first he wouldn't even stand still. He'd pull away or walk away. Sometimes he would interrupt me or act like he couldn't hear me."

"And what would you do?"

"I'd just keep right on with the Reprimand. When it was over, I went to bed. I did that every single night."

"And what happened?"

"Within weeks the boy was asking to use the car and coming home early."

The young woman was astonished. "Are you serious?" she asked.

"Absolutely," the woman answered, "very serious. In fact, I think that's how I got such good results. It was a serious situation. When I took it seriously and expressed my anger clearly, I got results. Remember, however," she added, "I went after the behavior, not after David."

The young woman nodded and said, "What a way to change behavior! But," she wondered, "does this whole process really take only a minute?"

"Usually," the daughter said. "And when it's over, it's over. A One Minute Reprimand doesn't last very long, but I can guarantee you, you don't forget it! And you don't want to make the same mistake again."

"I wonder," the visitor continued, "if The One Minute Mother ever makes mistakes?"

The daughter grinned and said, "Of course she does. That's part of what makes her so likable."

"Can you give me an example?"

"Well," said the daughter, "sometimes Mother would forget to do the last half of the Reprimand —the part where she would remind us that we were really good and worthwhile."

"I imagine that's easy to do," the visitor said, "especially if you're really upset with your child's behavior."

"It is. Anyway, whenever she did this, each of us would each remind her later that we would certainly like the last half—the nice half."

"And what would she do?" the visitor asked.

"She would laugh and say she got so carried away with reprimanding the behavior she forgot to praise the child. Then she would really exaggerate her words about how much she *loved* us, and how *highly* she thought of us as individuals in our own right, and how much *better* we were than our recent misbehavior, and what *fine* people we were, how *proud* she was of us, how . . .

"Until we'd finally say, 'OK, Mom, OK. I got it. I got it.'"

The young woman laughed loudly and said, "I love it! It sounds like part of being a One Minute Mother is to keep your sense of humor."

Liz nodded her agreement. "As Mother used to say, 'The best way for a mother to keep her sanity is to keep her sense of humor.'"

Just then, the young woman heard the sounds of laughter and play outside. "That's my boy David and his friends," Liz said.

"Do you mind if I talk with him?"

"Not at all. We now have open and honest communications in this family once again."

Then the woman added, "You know, someone once said, 'A family is a group of people irrationally committed to one another's well-being.' David and I are only a group of two but we really are a family again." Elizabeth Franklin was happy.

Leaving, the visitor said, "Thank you so much for what you have taught me today." She went outside to talk to the woman's son.

David excused himself from his friends to speak to the visitor. She asked about the incident with the car. He suggested they go for a walk.

"Every time I'd come home late with the car," he explained, "my mother would go through this 'drill.' She let me know how ticked off she was with me. I mean she really went bananas!

"That was bad enough," he continued. "But I mean I could put up with that. I'd just tune her out." Then he added, "Although I must admit, it wasn't always easy to ignore what she was saying.

"But then she would stop and put her arm around me and tell me how neat she really thought I was. What really got to me, though, was when she told me she respected me! She admired me! She loved me! Man, that was too much. I mean I really felt lousy about what I was doing. I remember one time I started to . . ." The boy stopped talking.

After a long pause, the boy said, "I guess I was glad that Mom finally stood up and told me how she really felt. I found out she didn't like what I was *doing* but she liked *me*.

"I know a lot of other kids' parents let them get away with whatever they want. But to tell you the truth, I don't think it makes them feel very good."

"You mean you think that the kids feel like their parents don't care about them or love them?"

"Yes," the boy confirmed. "We all know when we've done wrong. And we know lots of times the other person knows. When they ignore it, we feel ignored—like we don't matter.

"In fact," the young man continued, "I've learned that talking to somebody like this works out real well. Now when I'm angry or frustrated about what Mom is doing, she lets me express myself just as straight. And she thinks about what I tell her—because she knows how much I like it. It's a great two-way street."

The young woman walked along and thought about what the boy had said. Later she thanked him for talking with her and went to her car.

As she sat behind the steering wheel, she reflected on all that she had learned. Then she pulled out her notebook and wrote a summary of what she now knew about the One Minute Reprimand. She wrote it as though she herself were already a mother who was using the method successfully.

The One Minute Reprimand works well when:

1. I tell my children that I will let them know when their behavior is not acceptable to me; I ask them to do the same with respect to me.

The First Half of the Reprimand

2. I reprimand my children as *soon* as possible.
3. I tell my children *specifically* what is unacceptable to me.
4. I tell my children, in no uncertain terms, how I *feel* about what they have done.
5. I am silent for a few seconds—to let them *feel* my discomfort.

The Second Half of the Reprimand

6. I *touch* my children in a way that lets them know that I am on their side.
7. I remind my children that I know that each of them is a valuable and worthwhile person.
8. I simply tell my children that while I do not like their recent behavior, *I do like them.*
9. I signal the end of the Reprimand by hugging my children and telling them, "I love you!" My children and I realize that when the Reprimand is over—it's over!
10. I realize that while it may take me only a minute to reprimand my children with love, the benefits may last them for a *lifetime.*

That evening, the young woman's husband looked over her notes. He might not have believed in the effectiveness of the One Minute Reprimand if his wife had not seen the results personally. There was, however, no doubt about it. She knew it worked!

The young woman told her husband that she knew that everyone made mistakes now and then, including her. But she knew that if she ever received a One Minute Reprimand it would be fair because it would be a comment on her *behavior* and not on her *worth* as a person.

She thought about how much we—adults and children alike—like to be treated well as people.

As she later drove toward The One Minute Mother's attractive home, she kept thinking about the simplicity of One Minute Reprimanding.

All three secrets made sense—One Minute Goals, One Minute Praisings and One Minute Reprimands.

The young woman could easily see how communicating in this way would reduce stress in the family.

"But *why* do they work?" she wondered. "Why is The One Minute Mother so successful with her children?"

WHEN the young woman arrived at The Mother's home, it was early evening. The sun was setting and the streetlights had come on.

As she examined the home, she noticed things she hadn't seen on her first visit. She saw the well-groomed front lawn and the beautifully decorated entrance hall. She became aware of small details. Inside, the woman's home glowed—not with ordinary white light bulbs, but with the soft, flattering dawn-pink bulbs she had once seen in a decorator's home. The One Minute Mother had paid attention to the many little things that made life more enjoyable.

Her hostess greeted her with a warm smile and an immediate question. "Well, what did you discover during your expedition?"

"A great deal!" the visitor replied.

"Tell me what you've learned," the woman said eagerly.

"I found out why people call you The One Minute Mother. You set One Minute Goals with your children to make sure that they knew what you all wanted to see happen. You showed them what good performance looked like. You then tried to catch your children doing something right so you could give them a One Minute Praising. And then, finally, if they had the understanding and ability to know better, and they still did something that was clearly unacceptable to you, you gave them a One Minute Reprimand."

"What do you think about all that?" asked The One Minute Mother.

"To begin with," said the young woman, "I'm amazed at how simple it is. And yet it works—you get marvelous results. I'm convinced that it certainly worked for *you*."

"And it will work for you, too, if you are willing to *do* it," The Mother insisted.

"Perhaps," said the young woman, "but I would be more likely to do it if I could understand more about *why* it works."

"That's true of everyone. The more each of us understands something, the more apt we are to *use* it. I'd be happy, therefore, to tell you what I know. Where would you like me to start?"

"Well, I noticed when I visited each of your daughters that they seemed happy and full of energy. Does One Minute Parenting work because it takes so little time and energy? I mean . . . for example, did it really take only a minute to do all the things you needed to do as a parent?"

"No, of course not. It's just a way of saying that being an effective parent needn't be as time-consuming as you might think. It might take more than a minute to deal with some problems—that's just a symbolic term. But it does take only a minute to deal with a lot of situations.

"The real reason that I and my daughters—and any woman who chooses to be a One Minute Mother—have more energy is that we simply don't deal with our children the way most women do.

"Too many mothers are exhausted," the woman said, "because they use the 'housekeeping' method of parenting."

"What?"

"Most mothers still assume most of the responsibility for keeping the house clean—whether they do it themselves or oversee someone else doing it. They get the house clean just to catch up to where they already were—back to having a clean house again. They have the maddeningly frustrating feeling that they never really get ahead.

"And to make matters more tiring," The Mother continued, "many women act this way with their children.

"When their children are well behaved . . . or," The Mother added with a smile, "when they are just quietly out of sight, what do most mothers do?"

"Nothing," the young woman noted.

"Precisely," said The One Minute Mother. "Using the ineffective housekeeping method of child rearing, these mothers don't see any *need* for intervention at these times. As though good parenting were primarily solving problems or 'straightening out the kids.' To these women, parenting a well-behaved child would be like cleaning the house when the house is already clean."

"But what *would* you do with a well-behaved child?" asked the young woman.

"Think about what you have seen and heard over the last few days," The Mother suggested. "How much of the parenting time did my daughters spend dealing with children's behavioral problems?"

"Well, now that you mention it, not very much," the young woman said. "They spent most of their time setting goals with their children and then catching them doing things right."

"Right! Right!" The One Minute Mother said. Then she added with a wide grin, "Excuse the pun."

The visitor didn't see the humor. She admitted, "To tell you the truth, as I was visiting your daughters and learning about being a One Minute Mother, I wondered if I weren't living in a fairy tale. I mean it all seemed so positive and easy. It wasn't like anything I'd ever seen before."

The One Minute Mother nodded her agreement and said, "That's because most women don't know how easy it can be. They have been told over and over that being a parent is a difficult, complicated, confusing responsibility. They raise their children the way they have seen others do. They try to teach them when they are misbehaving—when the children are not feeling very good about themselves. That's when children—or any of us for that matter—are defensive and resistant. The time to teach a child, however, is when he is well behaved."

The visitor said, "I think I know what you are talking about. Maybe I could understand better, however, if I could get to some of my 'why' questions. Perhaps we could start with One Minute Goal Setting. Why does it work so well?"

"**Y**OU want to know why One Minute Goals work so well," The Mother said. "Fine.

"There are several reasons. Let me give you a few analogies that might help."

The woman went to the window and invited her visitor to come over and look out at the lawn.

"What would happen if golf balls were the color of grass?" The Mother asked.

The young woman smiled at such an idea. She thought for a moment and then said, "It probably wouldn't be as much fun to play golf."

"Why not?" The Mother asked.

"Because you'd spend too much time trying to find the ball somewhere in the grass. The ball would blend in with the grass and it would therefore be difficult to see.

"It's hard to find what you can't see," the young woman noted.

"What?" The One Minute Mother asked with a smile.

The young woman smiled too, knowing full well that The Mother was letting her discover things for herself. She said slowly, ". . . It's hard to find . . . what you can't see. . . ."

"Imagine, for a moment," The Mother suggested, "that you are a golfer. You are playing in an important game with a woman who usually plays as well as you. You are using golf balls that are exactly the same color as the grass you are playing on. The other person, however, is allowed to use nice, new, white balls."

The young woman laughed and said, "I don't think I'm going to like this game."

"Why not?"

"Because one of us has an unfair advantage. I don't think I'm going to do very well. In fact, I'm going to look bad."

"You *are* going to look bad," The Mother confirmed. "Especially when you compare yourself to another person who can easily see what she is looking for. She on the other hand, is going to enjoy herself."

"So," the young woman began, "you're telling me that the same thing is true with children. It's easier and more fun for them when they can see what they are shooting for."

"Exactly! Everyone likes to do well—to look good. Looking at your goals for a minute each day helps you *attain* your goals."

The Mother walked over to her desk. She pointed to a saying that she had placed over her work area. "Look at this," she said. "Wiser people than I have called this 'The Greatest Secret in the World.'"

*

*We Become
What We
Think About*

*

"This 'secret' has been known for a long time by a few people. Some of the most intelligent people down through the ages have disagreed on a lot of things. But all the great philosophers agree on this: We do indeed become what we think about.

"Modern scientists call it 'visualization'—seeing something as true in your mind before it actually exists. It sounds mystical to some. But it is just a good practical tool for success. As I said, some people learned it long ago. Shakespeare said, 'All things are ready if our minds be so.'"

"So," the young woman said, "One Minute Goals are really just an easy way to help children see what they would like to become."

"Yes. And they help more than just children. Written goals also help parents. One of the reasons that they help big people and little people is that they remove one of the biggest hurdles."

"Which is . . . ?"

"The scourge of modern times—anxiety," The One Minute Mother explained. "Children and parents are anxious today. They are not quite sure what to expect—of themselves or from each other.

"As you have probably experienced yourself, the greater the anxiety in your life, the poorer the performance."

"Can you give me an example of how and why anxiety gets in the way of good performance?" the visitor asked.

"Imagine if you will," The One Minute Mother began, "that you are asked to walk across a plank that is two inches thick, six inches wide, and thirty feet long.

"The plank is lying on the ground. At the end of the plank is a one-hundred-dollar bill. It is yours if you can just walk to the other end of the plank and pick it up. Do you think that you could do that— for one hundred dollars?"

"Certainly. That would be easy."

"OK. Now would you be willing to do the same thing with only one change? The plank is now stretched between two adjacent skyscrapers fifty stories high. There is no wind. Another hundred-dollar bill is lying on the other end of the plank. Are you willing to walk across and pick it up?"

The visitor grinned as she shook her head from side to side and said, "No way!"

"What if it were for five hundred dollars?"

"I wouldn't do it for a thousand dollars."

"Why wouldn't you?"

"Because I would be afraid I might fall," the visitor admitted. "Even if I tried, I'd probably freeze halfway across. My fear of falling would get in the way. I just couldn't do it."

"Precisely. Fear immobilizes people! And one of the most debilitating kinds of fear is anxiety. Anxiety is simply fear of the unknown.

"One Minute Goals work because they lower anxiety," The One Minute Mother noted. "They free children up to do better."

"Why and how does that work? And can you give me a practical example?"

The One Minute Mother smiled and said, "You really want to understand why One Minute Parenting works so well, don't you?"

"I really do!"

"All right. A classic example happened in London, during the Second World War. People were very much afraid of the bombs, which were falling fairly regularly on the city. Then, as the war was fading, the bombs tapered off. Finally they stopped. But the people continued to look skyward. They couldn't be sure if the bombs would fall again."

The visitor said, "It sounds like some homes I've been in. The kids never knew when the next bomb would drop."

"Well said! Now, if you were to go back and study the mental-health records of the English people during that time," The Mother said, "when do you think the people were the most distressed and paid the most visits to psychiatrists and psychologists? When the bombs were dropping? Or when they weren't dropping?"

"I'm not sure."

"English health professionals," the woman said, "saw more distraught people *after* the war. The real threat was over, of course.

"People were able to deal all right with their real fear. But they were unable to deal with their anxiety. Not knowing is unsettling."

"And not knowing," the young woman interjected, "has the same unsettling effect on children."

The One Minute Mother grinned and clapped her hands together with loud approval. "You understand!" she said.

The One Minute Mother leaned forward and poured each of them a fresh cup of coffee. It had grown cold in the heat of conversation.

"You listen very well," The One Minute Mother said. "And you *think* just as well.

"I feel very good telling someone like you what I know. I feel that it is worth my time. I feel that you are likely to *use* what you are learning. I am very pleased!"

The Mother stretched out and touched her visitor's arm in a gesture of approval and support.

The young woman beamed her appreciation. It felt good to be recognized by this woman.

The young woman paused to savor the feeling. Then she said, "I know that you just gave me a One Minute Praising. And I really enjoyed it. But what amazes me is that I feel so good about it. I know what you are doing and it still feels great!"

"Do you know why you feel good?" The Mother asked. "Because you honestly *felt* appreciated. And that's because you *were* appreciated."

The visitor began to speak but The One Minute Mother anticipated her question. "Let me guess," she said. "You wonder *why* praisings are so effective."

"You took the words right out of my mouth. Just why *are* One Minute Praisings so effective?"

"**O**NE Minute Praisings work," The Mother explained, "because they are so *natural.*"

"Natural?" the visitor asked.

"Yes. Look, for example, at two of the most natural events in a child's life: learning to walk and learning to talk. What do parents do when a child is learning to walk?"

The visitor thought for a moment and said, "Well, they stand the youngster up, hold her hands, and walk a few steps at a time with her."

"And what do they say to the youngster?"

"They exclaim over each tiny step, saying things like 'What a great walker!'"

"And then what happens one day when the youngster pulls herself up from a happy crawl across the living-room carpet to stand at the edge of the coffee table?"

The visitor smiled. "The parents literally drop everything else they are doing to cheer the great accomplishment."

"What do they do?" The Mother asked.

"They go to her and give her lots of hugs and kisses and say things like 'Would you look at you! Standing up! And all by yourself!' 'Aren't you terrific!' or 'What a great little girl!'"

"Exactly," The Mother agreed. "Now think about that for a minute. Does that sound familiar?"

The young woman paused and then said, "It sounds like a One Minute Praising."

"It *is* a One Minute Praising. And that is what parents normally do with their children when they are small.

"Now take it a few steps further," The Mother said, enjoying the pun. "What do the parents do next—after the child has learned to stand?"

"They hold out their arms and encourage their youngster to take a few daring steps in their direction. And of course they watch closely so they can keep the child from falling."

"Look at that for a moment," The Mother suggested. "The parents take the child in very small increments toward the eventual goal of walking. And with each little accomplishment along the way, what do they do?"

"They praise the youngster enthusiastically."

"Precisely! It's the natural way to help children learn to like themselves—to have high self-esteem."

The visitor understood. She said quietly, as though she were talking to herself, "The child learns and the parent enjoys."

"Yes. Praisings work," The Mother said, "because children learn *faster* and parents get *more* enjoyment.

"The same thing is true with learning to talk. Let's say you would like your child to ask for a drink when she is thirsty. I know you don't have a child yet, but what would happen if you waited until your child said the full sentence 'May I please have a drink, Mother?'"

"I think I'd have a dehydrated child."

The Mother smiled and said, "I think you're right. And what if you just waited until she said the word 'drink' perfectly before you gave her one?"

"I think I'd have the same problem."

"Sure. So what would you do?"

The young woman noted, "I don't think I'd wait until she could say the whole word perfectly."

"That's right! Let's say she motions to you that she is thirsty and she says only the last part of the word. She says, 'Ink, ink.'

"Remember," The Mother cautioned, "it's the *first* word she's ever said."

The young woman responded, "I think I'd probably get very excited. I'd give her a big hug and tell her what a big girl she was. In fact, to tell you the truth, I'd immediately get on the phone to her grandmother. My daughter would soon be saying, 'Ink, ink,' across America."

The Mother laughed and said, "In that case, you'd be very normal. And the great part is that your child would learn to speak more quickly— because you didn't wait until she did it perfectly right. You enthusiastically caught her doing something *approximately* right.

"In fact, you did something very important. You didn't wait until you knew the absolutely perfect way to parent your child yourself. You went ahead and did what you felt was right for you. And that is a critical part of being a successful parent.

"There's a thought I keep in mind whenever I am wondering personally if I can do a good job at something."

"What is that?" the young woman wanted to know.

"It's just this . . .

*

It Is More Important
For Me To Start Right Away
To Do The Right Thing

Than It Is To Wait
Until I Think I Can
Do It Just Right

*

"In fact," The Mother continued, "the more often you praise your children for doing something right—even if it's not perfect—the more quickly they begin to appreciate how good they are.

"We all need to be honestly appreciated, even if what we are doing doesn't always seem to be a big event in the eyes of the world.

"Now, of course, you don't want your ten-year-old child going into a restaurant and asking for a glass of 'ink.'"

The visitor smiled at the idea of such an untasty event.

"So you eventually encourage her a step at a time to do better. And each time she does, you feel like praising her. And before long she is talking.

"And let me compliment you, now that I think of it," The Mother said, "on hugging your child. You said that the first thing you would do when your child said her first word would be to hug her and praise her. That's great!"

"Is that important—the physical part?" the visitor asked.

"I mean, what if I have a big teenager who seems uncomfortable about being hugged. Just how important is touching as part of the One Minute Praising?"

"Touching is *very* important!" The Mother said. "In fact, there was an interesting study done once which dramatically shows the value of touching.

"A fifteenth-century emperor wanted to discover how people begin to speak. He wondered if they would speak if they never heard a spoken word. So he had infants taken away from their mothers and fathers and divided into two groups.

"The first group of infants was raised in much the normal way, the second group very differently.

"The nurses came robotlike into the nursery occasionally to clean and feed the children. Their visits were very brief. They said nothing and left. The children were, for all practical purposes, never touched. They just lay there month after month alone."

The young woman frowned and said, "That sounds to me more like a cruel experiment than a valid scientific study. I certainly wouldn't want to be one of those ignored babies."

"You're right. It *was* cruel. And what do you think happened to those children?"

"Well, to begin with," the young woman said, "I don't think they learned to talk very well. And furthermore, I don't think they grew up to be very happy adults."

"Why not?" The Mother asked.

"Because I think children need to be held and cuddled and talked to and cooed over and . . . in short, to be made to feel like they matter."

Then she asked, "What *did* happen to those children?"

"By the end of the year, they were all dead."

The young woman was shocked. She stared for a moment. Then she swallowed hard and asked, "What did you say?"

"I'm afraid," The Mother said gently, "you heard correctly. The first group of infants had the normal survival rate. But the second group, even though they had their basic physical needs met— like food, heat, and clothing—*all* died in a year."

"My God!" the young woman exclaimed. "That's inhuman!" She thought for a moment and asked, "Why did the children die?"

"Today's physicians and behavioral scientists have observed similar results," the woman explained, "in children who, for one reason or another, have also been neglected. From their observations of children—both sick and well— they believe that youngsters cannot thrive unless they are 'bonded.'"

"I don't understand," the young woman admitted.

"Well, none of us really understands it as well as we might want to," The Mother said. "But bonding is essentially the emotional attachment that occurs between an infant who is totally dependent on someone else for his survival and an adult who cares enough to nurture the child to the point where he can stand on his own.

"Apparently children need to be loved in order to grow—physically and emotionally. If children get very little love, they fail to *thrive*—physically or emotionally. If they get *no* love, they fail to *survive*."

"I had no idea that physical touching was so important," the young woman admitted.

"Touching is probably the most honest of all forms of communication," The Mother said. "And if it is honest, it is powerful.

"Many studies have shown the power of touching," The Mother noted. "In one, behavioral scientists intentionally left a dime in a public phone booth. As each person left the booth, he was approached and asked if he had found the dime.

"The people were approached in two ways. Each was asked, 'Excuse me. Did you find my dime?' Some people were lightly touched while the question was being asked; others were not."

"Was there any difference in the response?" the young woman asked.

"Yes, there was. Of the group that was not touched, fewer than fifty percent of the people admitted they had found the dime. Of those who were touched, over ninety percent gave the dime back—and with a smile!"

"That's terrific," the visitor said. "It looks like people feel warmer toward other people when they are touched—and they are willing to do more for them. Maybe that's why we use expressions like 'I was *touched* by what she did for me.'"

"Possibly. But remember," The Mother cautioned, "the more honest you are, the better it works.

"It is also interesting to note," The Mother pointed out, "that as important as physical touch is, you can also touch your child with your eyes— by simply paying attention to him or her. It is far more important than most parents realize.

"I still remind myself of this by doing something very simple and very important . . .

*

*I Take A Minute
Out Of My Day
Every Now And Then*

*To Look Into
The Faces
Of My Children*

*

"Children have a great need to be recognized," The Mother said. "And one of the most nurturing things a mother can do is to 'watch' and to praise.

"Mothers, of course, are supposed to be nurturing," The One Minute Mother added. "And I *enjoyed* nurturing my children.

"But there is something else just as important. I always wanted my children to remember that *I* needed to be nurtured too.

"So I asked my children to remember, when they honestly feel it, to give me praisings—to hug me. And to tell me that they appreciate what I am doing.

"I let them know that I really felt better," The Mother said, "whenever one of them came up to me and hugged me and said, *'You're a great mom. I love you, Mom!'*"

"And did they?" the young woman asked.

"Yes, they did. In fact, they still do!

"Do you know how I used to remind my children of this?"

"How?" the visitor inquired.

"I put a sign up on our refrigerator."

"OK. I'll bite," the young woman said with a smile. "What did the sign say?"

The Mother wrote it out on a piece of paper and handed it to the young woman.

*

Mothers
Are
People
Too

*

"I love it!" the young woman said. "It's something I'm going to remember.

"If praisings help children feel better about themselves," she continued, "then why not use the same thoughtful method to help parents feel better too. They certainly deserve it!

"It also gives the children a chance to learn how to *give* praisings as well as to receive them."

"And the children learn," The One Minute Mother said, "that the best part is that it will get great results. When parents are caught doing something right, they want to do more of it. I know I do!"

"It's amazing," the young woman said. "Now that I have a chance to listen to all that I have just learned and to think about it, I can certainly understand a good deal better why One Minute Praisings work so well with parents as well as with children."

She paused for a long moment, smiled, and then said, "One Minute Reprimands—why?"

The Mother returned her friendly smile and said, "I was wondering when you were going to get around to that."

"THERE are two basic reasons why One Minute Reprimands work so well," The Mother said. "They *reduce stress* and they *increase success.*"

"I don't understand," the visitor said. "I thought reprimands were used in stressful situations. Why do they *reduce* stress? I should think that they would escalate it."

"Let me tell you about my favorite ad on television," The Mother said.

The visitor smiled. She knew she was about to learn something.

"The ad is for a motor oil. A man holds up a can of high-quality oil which he suggests I buy. It will be well worth the investment of a few extra dollars, he says. He promises me a better-running car—I'll have a lot fewer problems."

Then The Mother said, "Do you have any idea just how *uninterested* I am in motor oil?"

The visitor laughed and said, "I know what you mean. I just want to get into my car and drive it—with no problems."

"Don't we all!" The Mother agreed. "In fact, what I really want to do is ignore the whole idea of taking care of my car. I just want a smooth-running car. But then this ad really gets to me."

"What happens?"

"This fellow leans in real close to the camera and says quietly, 'You can pay me now . . . or . . .'

"Then the scene cuts away to a shot of an engine being slowly lifted out of the car by a big crane or something and the fellow says, '. . . or you can pay me later!'"

The One Minute Mother laughed and said, "And, of course, that's true of so many things in life. We can pay a small price now. Or we can pay a big price later.

"One Minute Reprimands work because they help you pay a small price now—by dealing immediately with unacceptable behavior—and avoid paying a big price later—like the kind of serious problems many families must face."

"And, of course, when the big trouble comes," the young woman noted, "it's not just the child's problem; it affects the entire family."

"That's very true.

"Let's stay with the car and oil example," The Mother suggested. "The normal running of a car causes wear and tear on the engine parts. The oil lubricates the parts and lets them slide more easily over one another—thus reducing the normal stress. When we ignore the oil, however, we increase the stress inside the engine, and eventually things break down.

"And the same is true with our children," The Mother explained. "The normal running of lives includes the wear and tear of mistakes. There are going to be problems. That's part of living.

"When we ignore the problems, they get worse!

"It's not the problems that are the problem. It's the way we handle the problems," The Mother continued. "And that is what I like about using One Minute Reprimands. They are an attractive way to handle an unattractive situation."

"How can something like a Reprimand be attractive?" the visitor asked.

"Before I answer that," The One Minute Mother said, "let me ask you a question: What is a child's greatest fear?"

"I don't know," the visitor responded.

"Think about yourself—when you were a child. What was yours?"

The young woman thought for only a moment. "I can remember when I was very little," she said. "I used to think I was abnormal or something because I was afraid that my parents would leave me behind—like in a supermarket or something. And I wouldn't be able to find my way home.

"When they went out at night and I was with a baby-sitter, I would worry about whether or not they would come home. I know that sounds strange but I can still remember the feeling."

"And it scared you, didn't it?"

"It really did. Of course, my mom and dad were great. They never left me. But I still worried about it a lot."

"You are very normal. *Abandonment* is indeed the greatest fear a child has!

"And that is why a One Minute Reprimand will work so well with your children. In spite of the fact that they have misbehaved, perhaps very badly, *they* are not rejected—not abandoned.

"The *key* to a mother's success with a One Minute Reprimand is that she distinguishes between a child's behavior and a child's worth.

"Your reprimanded child feels that her recent *behavior* is not acceptable, but that *she* always is."

The young woman said, "That's terrific! So the child feels safe."

"Yes," The Mother confirmed. "That's why the second part of the Reprimand is so important."

"The part where you remind the child that she is a good person and that you really love her?"

"Yes, that is the critical part of any good Reprimand."

"Why is it so important?" the young woman wanted to know. "What if a mother just tells her child 'in no uncertain terms' how upset she is with the behavior—and nothing more?"

"That is precisely what most mothers do. And it usually doesn't work—as you may have observed. It just makes the child more defensive and resentful.

"It seems like a very little difference," The Mother noted. "But that very little difference makes a very *big* difference."

The visitor smiled and said, "Like the two women in the telephone booth."

It was The Mother's turn to ask, "What?"

"One woman has nine pennies . . ."

The Mother smiled and said, ". . . and the other woman has a dime!"

The visitor nodded and said, "And that very little difference makes a very big difference."

"That's a marvelous example," The Mother said.

"So," the visitor summarized, "you are saying that the difference between success and failure is whether or not your reprimanded child, who may feel bad about getting a reprimand for bad behavior, feels good about *herself* or not."

"Absolutely right!" The Mother replied. "And do you understand why that is so important?"

"I'm not really sure," the young woman said.

"What happens when you squeeze an orange?" The Mother asked. "What do you get?"

"Orange juice," the visitor answered. She thought, "Here we go again." She loved the way The Mother brought out of her what she already knew but was not yet aware of. She felt good.

"Of course," The Mother said. "Could you ever get grapefruit juice?"

"No, of course not. Not out of an orange."

"What if we squeezed harder?"

The visitor laughed and said, "That would be a waste of our time. We already know what's going to come out."

"Think about what you just said," The One Minute Mother suggested. "We know, don't we, that whenever we put pressure on something, what comes out is what's already inside.

"When pressure is put on one of our children, especially peer pressure, what comes out—our child's behavior—is what's already inside—our child's self-esteem.

"Our job as parents is simply," The Mother said, "to raise children who *believe* in themselves.

"Children who really believe in themselves like themselves. And they begin to help raise themselves. That's when the job gets a lot easier.

"As you have heard several times since you began to discover the three secrets of One Minute Parenting, children who like themselves like to behave themselves. They grow into happy and productive adults. They are a joy to parent."

Then The Mother added, "Of course, the most important parent is not you."

The startled young woman said, "I hope you're not going to say it's the father."

The Mother laughed out loud. "No! One parent is as important as the other. In fact, one of the best things about One Minute Parenting is that it works whether two parents are using it or only one.

"The most important parent for your children, however," The Mother explained, "is not you, but the 'internal parent' who develops in each of your children. The child's *internal* parent will go everywhere with her and will help her with all her decisions.

"What you want is not discipline for your child, but *self*-discipline. When she is first learning, the discipline you show your child is a good model for her to copy. But it is only the first step on the road to discovering something far more important—an invaluable sense of *personal* discipline.

*

What's Important As A Parent
Is Not So Much
What Happens
When You're There

It's What Happens
When You're Not *There*

*

"My children's sense of good judgment develops better when they know how they're really doing."

"Does it work both ways?" the young woman asked. "I mean, did your children get to tell you how they felt about what you did?"

"Absolutely!" The One Minute Mother answered. "And that's important. If children bury their anger or frustration about something they think isn't right at home, they become a pain in the neck to be around. They mope around the house, they don't listen, they act resentful." She smiled and said, "You'd think they were the last of the martyrs.

"Sometimes I got busy with so many other things that I overlooked something that was really important to the children. To them it may have seemed as if I didn't care about them.

"However, after they put things frankly out on the table, we usually discovered that all we had was a communications problem, not a caring problem."

"I gather," the young woman said, "that it didn't remain a problem very long."

"No, it didn't. While I made it very clear that I expected my children to respect me, they could tell me whatever they felt—as long as they didn't attack me as a person. When they respected *me,* I listened to what they were saying."

"So you really listened to your children."

"Yes. I liked them to listen to me. And the best way to get my children to listen was . . ."

"To listen to them," the visitor noted.

The Mother smiled and said, "Albert Schweitzer, I think, said it best.

*

Children Learn
In Three Ways

By Example
By Example
And . . .

*

"By example," the young woman added.

The Mother said, "You've got it. And one of the best examples I can set is that it is safe for us to get angry. The children see that feelings, even negative feelings, can be expressed safely—if they are expressed *early,* when they are still small."

The visitor said, "I would think expressing how you feel would also help stressed mothers avoid the nightmare of child abuse.

"I mean, I understand one of the biggest reasons mothers surprisingly abuse their children— physically or emotionally—is that they let things build up in them to where they can't take things anymore and unexpectedly explode."

"That's a very important point. And using nonviolent discipline like a One Minute Reprimand does two things: It lets you release your feelings *and* nourish your child."

"At the same time!" the visitor noted. "And the fabulous part is that a One Minute Mother needn't feel *guilty.* She doesn't have to worry about her children growing up feeling bad about themselves. She is free of the usual guilt most mothers have. She knows she has nourished her children's *self-esteem.* And that this will carry them on to a successful life—independent of their parents.

"Maybe you would find this interesting," the young woman continued, as she pointed to her notebook. "It's a plaque I've created to remind me of how setting *goals*—the One Minute Goals— and delivering *consequences*—the Praisings and Reprimands—affect behavior."

*

Goals
Begin
Behaviors

Consequences
Maintain
Behaviors

*

"That's very good!" The Mother exclaimed.

"Do you think so?" the young woman asked, wanting to hear the compliment again.

The Mother said, "I don't mean to be rude to you. But I do not have time to repeat myself."

Just when the young woman thought she would be praised, she felt she was now in for a mild One Minute Reprimand, something she wanted to avoid.

The bright young woman kept a straight face and said simply, "What?"

They looked at each other for only a moment and then they both burst out laughing.

"I like you," The One Minute Mother said. "You have a good sense of humor. You want to learn to do the right thing for yourself and your children, but you do not take yourself too seriously.

"Tell me," she added, "when are you going to have your baby?"

"In three months," the visitor replied.

The One Minute Mother said, "You're going to be a fine mother. Your child will be one of the lucky ones!"

As the women said their good-byes, they gave each other a long warm hug of mutual admiration and respect. They parted each the better for it.

Over the next several years, the young woman began to use what she now knew. And, of course, it paid off beautifully.

Because, eventually, the inevitable happened.

SHE became a One Minute Mother.

She became a One Minute Mother not because of what she knew but because of what she *did*.

She encouraged One Minute Goal Setting.

She gave One Minute Praisings.

She applied One Minute Reprimands.

She knew, of course, that it took longer than a minute here and there to be a good mother. But she soon learned that using these three ways to communicate with her children improved every minute she spent with them.

She hugged her children, spoke the simple truth, expressed her feelings clearly, and laughed often.

And, perhaps most important of all, she encouraged each of her children to use the same three methods of communications with her.

She had even created a "Game" summary of One Minute Parenting. She gave a copy to each of her children—to remind them that, while life was a priceless adventure to be valued and respected, it was also a game to be enjoyed.

THE ONE MINUTE MOTHER'S "GAME PLAN"

*I Teach My Children to Like Themselves
and to Like to Behave Themselves.
And I Enjoy Myself in the Process.*

- I set goals, and praise and reprimand behavior.
- I speak the simple truth and express my feelings clearly.
- I hug my children and laugh often.

AND I ENCOURAGE MY CHILDREN TO DO AS I DO.

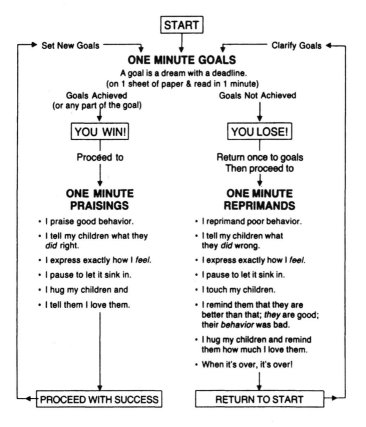

MANY years later, the once-young woman looked back on the time when she had first heard of the principles of One Minute Parenting. She was glad she had written down what she had learned from The One Minute Mother.

She had put her notes into a little book and had given copies to many people.

She remembered Mr. Merrick, the man from The Mother's old neighborhood, telephoning her to say, "I can't thank you enough. I am *using* the three secrets of One Minute Parenting myself. And it's been a big *improvement* for my family!

"You might like to know," he added, "that I've experienced several situations that are unique to *fathers*. The principles are the same, but I've discovered that some differences exist for men."

"That's very interesting!" she said. "Now that you mention it, I recall the original One Minute Mother saying that she learned a great deal from a man in her neighborhood—someone they called The One Minute Father.

"You might like to talk with him about the difference between how mothers and fathers raise children. It might be a big help to you."

He said he would follow up on it. Then he thanked her again and hung up.

She was pleased that other fathers were using One Minute Parenting as well.

As she thought back on the past, she smiled. She remembered how much she had learned from the original One Minute Mother, and she was grateful.

The new mother was also happy that she could take the knowledge one step further. By giving copies to family, friends, and neighbors, she had solved several practical problems.

Almost everyone who knew her knew "up front" what she was doing and why.

They could also see *why* the seemingly simple One Minute Parenting techniques—Goals, Praisings, and Reprimands—worked so well.

Every person who had his own copy of the text could read and reread it at his own pace until he could understand it and put it to good use himself. The mother knew full well the very practical advantage of the repetition in learning anything new.

Sharing the knowledge in this simple and honest way had, of course, saved her a good deal of time. And it had certainly made life easier.

Many of the others in the family and in the neighborhood had become One Minute Parents themselves. And they, in turn, had done the same for others.

The family had become happier and the neighborhood a more enjoyable place to live.

As she sat in her home, the new One Minute Mother realized what a fortunate individual she was. She had given herself the gift of getting greater results in less time.

She had time to think and to plan—to give her family the kind of help it needed.

She had time to exercise and stay healthy.

She knew she did not experience the daily emotional and physical stress other mothers subject themselves to.

And she knew that many of the other people who knew her enjoyed the same benefits.

The woman had, of course, shared the three secrets with her husband, who had also begun to use them. They enjoyed supporting each other in their mutual efforts to raise their children.

In fact, they used their knowledge in their own relationship. And it had helped.

Their children had learned to like themselves and they liked to behave themselves.

They had avoided the problems too many other families knew—an increasing sense of frustration and failure. They had done more than avoid the common pain. They had experienced a rare pleasure. They knew the comfort of a happy home.

Then the mother went outside and walked about her backyard. She was deep in thought.

She felt good about herself—as a person and as a mother.

She was glad that she had begun to use new ways to communicate—even though it seemed at first that she wasn't being herself. She remembered that when she was first changing her tennis stroke, it hadn't seemed like her either. But with practice the new skills became a natural part of her.

Now, caring about her family enough to change her own behavior had paid off handsomely. She had the love and affection of every member of her family.

She knew she had become an effective mother because her children had learned to like themselves and behave themselves—and she had enjoyed *her*self.

SUDDENLY she heard the voice of one of her grown children who was visiting. He was calling through an open window, "Sorry to interrupt you, Mom. But there is a young man on the phone. He wants to know if he can come and talk to you and Dad about the way you raised your children."

The new One Minute Mother was pleased. She knew that more men were taking a greater interest in the lives of their families. And that some of them were as keen to learn about effective parenting as she had been.

The mother's family was happy and productive. They enjoyed one another. And so did those who knew them. It felt good to be in her position.

"Come any time," she heard herself telling the caller.

And soon she and her husband found themselves talking with a bright young man. "We're glad to share our parenting secrets with you," the new One Minute Mother said, as she showed the visitor to a chair. "We will make only one request of you."

"What is that?" the visitor asked.

"Simply," the parent began, "that you . . .

*

Share It With Others

*

**the
end**

Acknowledgments

Over the years I have learned a great deal from many individuals. I would like to acknowledge and give a public praising to the following people:

A Special Praising to:
Dr. Gerald Nelson, the originator of the One Minute Scolding, for what he taught me about separating behavior and personal worth.

And to:
Dr. Kenneth Blanchard for what he taught me about so many things, including personal humor and prosperity.

Dr. Dorothy Briggs, for what she taught me about a child's self-esteem.

Dr. Thomas Connellan for what he taught me about demonstrating positive reinforcement.

Vernon Johnson for what he taught me about crisis intervention.

Dr. Charles McCormick for what he taught me about honesty and touching.

Earl Nightingale for what he taught me about the Greatest Secret in the World.

Dr. Carl Rogers for what he taught me about personal honesty and openness.

Dr. R. James Steffen for what he taught me about the importance of doing what's more important now.

Dr. Thomas Gordon for what he taught me about listening and cooperating.

Nelson Burton, Sr., and *Nelson Burton, Jr.*, for what they taught me about winning.

About the Author

Spencer Johnson, M.D., is an internationally bestselling author whose books help millions of people discover simple truths they can use to have healthier lives with more success and less stress.

He is the originator and coauthor of *The One Minute Manager®*, the #1 *New York Times* bestseller, written with legendary management consultant Kenneth Blanchard, Ph.D. The book continues to appear on business bestseller lists and has become the most popular management method in the world.

Dr. Johnson has written many bestsellers, including five other books in the *One Minute®* series: *The One Minute $ales Person*, *The One Minute Mother"*, *The One Minute Father"*, *One Minute for Yourself"*, and *The One Minute Teacher"; Yes or No;* the popular *ValueTales"* children's books; and the perennial gift favorite, *The Precious Present.*

His education includes a B.A. in psychology from the University of Southern California, an M.D. degree from the Royal College of Surgeons, and medical clerkships at Harvard Medical School and The Mayo Clinic.

Dr. Johnson was medical director of communications for Medtronic, the inventors of cardiac pacemakers; research physician at The Institute for Inter-Disciplinary Studies, a think tank; and consultant to the Center for the Study of the Person, and to the School of Medicine, University of California.

His books have been featured often in the media, including CNN, *Today, Larry King Live, Time* magazine, *USA Today, The Wall Street Journal*, and United Press International.

There are more than eleven million copies of Spencer Johnson's books in print in twenty-six languages.

Lightning Source UK Ltd.
Milton Keynes UK
25 June 2010

156081UK00002B/84/P